MW00808448

My Personal

PRAYER
MAP
TRACKER

• • • • •

BARBOUR
PUBLISHING

© 2021 by Barbour Publishing, Inc.

Print ISBN (Women's Edition) 978-1-64352-869-4

All rights reserved. No part of this publication may be reproduced or transmitted for commercial purposes, except for brief quotations in printed reviews, without written permission of the publisher.

Churches and other noncommercial interests may reproduce portions of this book without the express written permission of Barbour Publishing, provided that the text does not exceed 500 words or 5 percent of the entire book, whichever is less, and that the text is not material quoted from another publisher. When reproducing text from this book, include the following credit line: "From *My Personal Prayer Map Tracker*, published by Barbour Publishing, Inc. Used by permission."

Scriptures taken from the Holy Bible, New International Version®. niv®. Copyright © 1973, 1978, 1984, 2011 by Biblica, Inc.™ Used by permission. All rights reserved worldwide.

Published by Barbour Publishing, Inc., 1810 Barbour Drive, Uhrichsville, Ohio 44683, www.barbourbooks.com

Our mission is to inspire the world with the life-changing message of the Bible.

 Member of the
Evangelical Christian
Publishers Association

Printed in China.

WHAT DOES PRAYER LOOK LIKE? . . .

● ● ● ● ●

Get ready to more fully experience the power of prayer in your everyday life with this creative prayer map tracker. . .where every colorful page will guide you to write out your prayer requests, answers to prayer, prayers you're waiting to have answered, and your prayer for the day. . .which then creates a specific map that you can track as you spend time each day in quiet conversation with the heavenly Father. (Be sure to record the date on each one of your prayer maps so you can look back over time and see how God has continued to work in your life!)

My Personal Prayer Map Tracker will not only encourage you to spend time talking with your heavenly Creator about the things that matter most. . .it will also help you build a healthy spiritual habit of continual prayer for life.

DATE ▶

PRAYER REQUESTS:

....
....
....
....
....
....
....
....
....

ANSWERS TO PRAYER:

....
....
....
....
....
....
....
....
....

MY PRAYER FOR TODAY...

....
....
....
....
....
....
....
....
....
....
....
....
....
....
....

AMEN.

PATIENTLY WAITING FOR...

....
....
....
....
....
....
....
....
....
....
....
....
....
....
....

Thank You, Lord,
for hearing my prayers!

*In every situation, by prayer
and petition, with thanksgiving,
present your requests to God.*

PHILIPPIANS 4:6

DATE ▶

PRAYER REQUESTS:

....
....
....
....
....
....
....
....
....

ANSWERS TO PRAYER:

....
....
....
....
....
....
....
....
....

MY PRAYER FOR TODAY...

....
....
....
....
....
....
....
....
....
....
....
....
....

AMEN.

PATIENTLY WAITING FOR...

....
....
....
....
....
....
....
....
....
....
....
....

Thank You, Lord,
for hearing my prayers!

*If we ask anything according
to [God's] will, he hears us.*
1 JOHN 5:14

DATE ▶

PRAYER REQUESTS:

....
....
....
....
....
....
....
....
....

ANSWERS TO PRAYER:

....
....
....
....
....
....
....
....
....
....

MY PRAYER FOR TODAY...

....
....
....
....
....
....
....
....
....
....
....
....
....
....

AMEN.

PATIENTLY WAITING FOR...

....
....
....
....
....
....
....
....
....
....
....
....
....

Thank You, Lord,
for hearing my prayers!

Devote yourselves to prayer.
COLOSSIANS 4:2

DATE ▶

PRAYER REQUESTS:

....
....
....
....
....
....
....
....
....

ANSWERS TO PRAYER:

....
....
....
....
....
....
....
....
....
....

MY PRAYER FOR TODAY...

....
....
....
....
....
....
....
....
....
....
....
....
....
....
....

AMEN.

PATIENTLY WAITING FOR...

....
....
....
....
....
....
....
....
....
....
....
....

Thank You, Lord,
for hearing my prayers!

*"Whatever you ask for in prayer,
believe that you have received it,
and it will be yours."*
MARK 11:24

DATE ▶

PRAYER REQUESTS:

....
....
....
....
....
....
....
....
....
....

ANSWERS TO PRAYER:

....
....
....
....
....
....
....
....
....
....
....

MY PRAYER FOR TODAY...

....

....

....

....

....

....

....

....

....

....

....

....

AMEN.

PATIENTLY WAITING FOR...

....

....

....

....

....

....

....

....

....

....

....

Thank You, Lord, for hearing my prayers!

"You will call on me and come and pray to me, and I will listen to you."

JEREMIAH 29:12

DATE ▶

PRAYER REQUESTS:

....

....

....

....

....

....

....

....

ANSWERS TO PRAYER:

....

....

....

....

....

....

....

....

....

....

....

MY PRAYER FOR TODAY...

....
....
....
....
....
....
....
....
....
....
....
....

AMEN.

PATIENTLY WAITING FOR...

....
....
....
....
....
....
....
....
....
....
....
....
....
....
....
....

Thank You, Lord,
for hearing my prayers!

Be. . .faithful in prayer.
ROMANS 12:12

DATE ▶

PRAYER REQUESTS:

....
....
....
....
....
....
....
....

ANSWERS TO PRAYER:

....
....
....
....
....
....
....
....
....
....

MY PRAYER FOR TODAY...

....
....
....
....
....
....
....
....
....
....
....
....
....

AMEN.

PATIENTLY WAITING FOR...

....
....
....
....
....
....
....
....
....
....
....
....
....

Thank You, Lord,
for hearing my prayers!

The LORD is near to all who call on him.
PSALM 145:18

DATE ▶

PRAYER REQUESTS:

....
....
....
....
....
....
....
....
....

ANSWERS TO PRAYER:

....
....
....
....
....
....
....
....
....
....

MY PRAYER FOR TODAY...

....

....

....

....

....

....

....

....

....

....

....

AMEN.

PATIENTLY WAITING FOR...

....

....

....

....

....

....

....

....

....

....

....

Thank You, Lord,
for hearing my prayers!

"Call to me and I will answer you."

JEREMIAH 33:3

DATE ▶

PRAYER REQUESTS:

....

....

....

....

....

....

....

....

ANSWERS TO PRAYER:

....

....

....

....

....

....

....

....

....

....

MY PRAYER FOR TODAY...

....
....
....
....
....
....
....
....
....
....
....
....
....
....
....

AMEN.

PATIENTLY WAITING FOR...

....
....
....
....
....
....
....
....
....
....
....
....

Thank You, Lord,
for hearing my prayers!

*"When you pray, go into your room,
close the door and pray to your Father,
who is unseen. Then your Father, who sees
what is done in secret, will reward you."*

MATTHEW 6:6

DATE ▶

PRAYER REQUESTS:

....
....
....
....
....
....
....
....
....

ANSWERS TO PRAYER:

....
....
....
....
....
....
....
....
....
....
....

MY PRAYER FOR TODAY...

....
....
....
....
....
....
....
....
....
....
....
....
....

AMEN.

PATIENTLY WAITING FOR...

....
....
....
....
....
....
....
....
....
....
....
....
....

Thank You, Lord,
for hearing my prayers!

*If we know that he hears us—
whatever we ask—we know that
we have what we asked of him.*
1 JOHN 5:15

PRAYER REQUESTS:

....

....

....

....

....

....

....

....

....

ANSWERS TO PRAYER:

....

....

....

....

....

....

....

....

....

....

MY PRAYER FOR TODAY...

....

....

....

....

....

....

....

....

....

....

....

AMEN.

PATIENTLY WAITING FOR...

....

....

....

....

....

....

....

....

....

....

....

....

....

Thank You, Lord,
for hearing my prayers!

*The prayer of a righteous person
is powerful and effective.*

JAMES 5:16

DATE ▶

PRAYER REQUESTS:

....

....

....

....

....

....

....

....

....

ANSWERS TO PRAYER:

....

....

....

....

....

....

....

....

....

....

MY PRAYER FOR TODAY...

....
....
....
....
....
....
....
....
....
....
....
....
....

AMEN.

PATIENTLY WAITING FOR...

....
....
....
....
....
....
....
....
....
....
....
....
....
....

Thank You, Lord,
for hearing my prayers!

*When you ask, you must believe
and not doubt, because the one
who doubts is like a wave of the sea,
blown and tossed by the wind.*

JAMES 1:6

DATE ▶

PRAYER REQUESTS:

....
....
....
....
....
....
....
....

ANSWERS TO PRAYER:

....
....
....
....
....
....
....
....
....
....

MY PRAYER FOR TODAY...

....
....
....
....
....
....
....
....
....
....
....
....
....
....

AMEN.

PATIENTLY WAITING FOR...

....
....
....
....
....
....
....
....
....
....
....
....
....
....
....

Thank You, Lord,
for hearing my prayers!

"Whatever you ask in my name
the Father will give you."
JOHN 15:16

DATE ▶

PRAYER REQUESTS:

....
....
....
....
....
....
....
....
....
....

ANSWERS TO PRAYER:

....
....
....
....
....
....
....
....
....
....
....

MY PRAYER FOR TODAY...

....

....

....

....

....

....

....

....

....

....

....

AMEN.

PATIENTLY WAITING FOR...

....

....

....

....

....

....

....

....

....

....

....

....

Thank You, Lord,
for hearing my prayers!

*"If you believe, you will receive
whatever you ask for in prayer."*
MATTHEW 21:22

DATE ▶

PRAYER REQUESTS:

....
....
....
....
....
....
....
....
....
....

ANSWERS TO PRAYER:

....
....
....
....
....
....
....
....
....
....

MY PRAYER FOR TODAY...

....
....
....
....
....
....
....
....
....
....
....

AMEN.

PATIENTLY WAITING FOR...

....
....
....
....
....
....
....
....
....
....
....
....

Thank You, Lord,
for hearing my prayers!

In the morning, LORD, you hear my voice;
in the morning I lay my requests before
you and wait expectantly.
PSALM 5:3

DATE ▶

PRAYER REQUESTS:

....
....
....
....
....
....
....
....
....

ANSWERS TO PRAYER:

....
....
....
....
....
....
....
....
....
....

MY PRAYER FOR TODAY...

....
....
....
....
....
....
....
....
....
....
....

AMEN.

PATIENTLY WAITING FOR...

....
....
....
....
....
....
....
....
....
....
....
....

Thank You, Lord,
for hearing my prayers!

*LORD, hear my prayer, listen to my cry
for mercy; in your faithfulness and
righteousness come to my relief.*

PSALM 143:1

DATE ▶

PRAYER REQUESTS:

....

....

....

....

....

....

....

....

....

ANSWERS TO PRAYER:

....

....

....

....

....

....

....

....

....

....

MY PRAYER FOR TODAY...

....

....

....

....

....

....

....

....

....

....

....

AMEN.

PATIENTLY WAITING FOR...

....

....

....

....

....

....

....

....

....

....

....

....

Thank You, Lord,
for hearing my prayers!

*"Watch and pray so that you will
not fall into temptation."*
MATTHEW 26:41

DATE ▶

PRAYER REQUESTS:

....

....

....

....

....

....

....

....

....

ANSWERS TO PRAYER:

....

....

....

....

....

....

....

....

....

....

PATIENTLY WAITING FOR...

....
....
....
....
....
....
....
....
....
....
....
....
....
....

MY PRAYER FOR TODAY...

....
....
....
....
....
....
....
....
....
....
....
....

AMEN.

Thank You, Lord,
for hearing my prayers!

*May these words of my mouth
and this meditation of my heart
be pleasing in your sight, LORD,
my Rock and my Redeemer.*

PSALM 19:14

DATE ▶

PRAYER REQUESTS:

....

....

....

....

....

....

....

....

ANSWERS TO PRAYER:

....

....

....

....

....

....

....

....

....

....

MY PRAYER FOR TODAY...

....

....

....

....

....

....

....

....

....

....

....

....

....

....

AMEN.

PATIENTLY WAITING FOR...

....

....

....

....

....

....

....

....

....

....

Thank You, Lord, for hearing my prayers!

"For the eyes of the Lord are on the righteous and his ears are attentive to their prayer."
1 PETER 3:12

DATE ▶

PRAYER REQUESTS:

....

....

....

....

....

....

....

....

ANSWERS TO PRAYER:

....

....

....

....

....

....

....

....

....

MY PRAYER FOR TODAY...

....
....
....
....
....
....
....
....
....
....
....
....
....

AMEN.

PATIENTLY WAITING FOR...

....
....
....
....
....
....
....
....
....
....
....
....

Thank You, Lord,
for hearing my prayers!

*"Love your enemies and pray for
those who persecute you."*
MATTHEW 5:44

DATE ▶

PRAYER REQUESTS:

....
....
....
....
....
....
....
....
....

ANSWERS TO PRAYER:

....
....
....
....
....
....
....
....
....
....

MY PRAYER FOR TODAY...

....

....

....

....

....

....

....

....

....

....

....

....

AMEN.

PATIENTLY WAITING FOR...

....

....

....

....

....

....

....

....

....

....

....

Thank You, Lord,
for hearing my prayers!

*"When you stand praying, if you hold
anything against anyone, forgive them,
so that your Father in heaven may
forgive you your sins."*

MARK 11:25

DATE ▶

PRAYER REQUESTS:

....
....
....
....
....
....
....
....

ANSWERS TO PRAYER:

....
....
....
....
....
....
....
....
....
....

MY PRAYER FOR TODAY...

....

....

....

....

....

....

....

....

....

....

....

....

AMEN.

PATIENTLY WAITING FOR...

....

....

....

....

....

....

....

....

....

....

....

....

....

Thank You, Lord, for hearing my prayers!

"Everyone who calls on the name of the Lord will be saved."
Acts 2:21

DATE ▶

PRAYER REQUESTS:

ANSWERS TO PRAYER:

MY PRAYER FOR TODAY...

....

....

....

....

....

....

....

....

....

....

....

....

....

AMEN.

PATIENTLY WAITING FOR...

....

....

....

....

....

....

....

....

....

....

....

....

....

Thank You, Lord,
for hearing my prayers!

*Hear my cry for help, my King
and my God, for to you I pray.*
PSALM 5:2

DATE ▶

PRAYER REQUESTS:

....
....
....
....
....
....
....
....

ANSWERS TO PRAYER:

....
....
....
....
....
....
....
....
....
....

MY PRAYER FOR TODAY...

....
....
....
....
....
....
....
....
....
....
....
....
....
....

AMEN.

PATIENTLY WAITING FOR...

....
....
....
....
....
....
....
....
....
....
....
....
....

Thank You, Lord,
for hearing my prayers!

By day the Lord directs his love,
at night his song is with me—
a prayer to the God of my life.

PSALM 42:8

DATE ▶

PRAYER REQUESTS:

....
....
....
....
....
....
....
....
....

ANSWERS TO PRAYER:

....
....
....
....
....
....
....
....
....
....

PATIENTLY WAITING FOR...

....
....
....
....
....
....
....
....
....
....
....
....
....

MY PRAYER FOR TODAY...

....
....
....
....
....
....
....
....
....
....
....
....
....
....

AMEN.

Thank You, Lord,
for hearing my prayers!

*Praise be to God, who has not rejected
my prayer or withheld his love from me!*
PSALM 66:20

DATE ▶

PRAYER REQUESTS:

....
....
....
....
....
....
....
....
....

ANSWERS TO PRAYER:

....
....
....
....
....
....
....
....
....

MY PRAYER FOR TODAY...

....

....

....

....

....

....

....

....

....

....

....

....

AMEN.

PATIENTLY WAITING FOR...

....

....

....

....

....

....

....

....

....

....

....

....

Thank You, Lord,
for hearing my prayers!

*But I pray to you, LORD, in the time of
your favor; in your great love, O God,
answer me with your sure salvation.*

PSALM 69:13

DATE ▶

PRAYER REQUESTS:

....
....
....
....
....
....
....
....
....

ANSWERS TO PRAYER:

....
....
....
....
....
....
....
....
....
....

MY PRAYER FOR TODAY...

....
....
....
....
....
....
....
....
....
....
....

AMEN.

PATIENTLY WAITING FOR...

....
....
....
....
....
....
....
....
....
....
....
....

Thank You, Lord,
for hearing my prayers!

The prayer of the upright pleases [the Lord].
PROVERBS 15:8

DATE ▶

PRAYER REQUESTS:

....
....
....
....
....
....
....
....
....

ANSWERS TO PRAYER:

....
....
....
....
....
....
....
....
....
....
....

MY PRAYER FOR TODAY...

....
....
....
....
....
....
....
....
....
....
....
....
....
....

AMEN.

PATIENTLY WAITING FOR...

....
....
....
....
....
....
....
....
....
....
....
....
....

Thank You, Lord,
for hearing my prayers!

*I will tell of the kindnesses of the LORD,
the deeds for which he is to be praised,
according to all the LORD has done for us.*
ISAIAH 63:7

DATE ▶

PRAYER REQUESTS:

....

....

....

....

....

....

....

....

ANSWERS TO PRAYER:

....

....

....

....

....

....

....

....

....

MY PRAYER FOR TODAY...

....

....

....

....

....

....

....

....

....

....

....

....

....

AMEN.

PATIENTLY WAITING FOR...

....

....

....

....

....

....

....

....

....

....

....

....

....

Thank You, Lord,
for hearing my prayers!

*Oh, look on us, we pray,
for we are all your people.*
ISAIAH 64:9

DATE ▶

PRAYER REQUESTS:

....
....
....
....
....
....
....
....
....

ANSWERS TO PRAYER:

....
....
....
....
....
....
....
....
....
....

MY PRAYER FOR TODAY...

....

....

....

....

....

....

....

....

....

....

....

....

AMEN.

PATIENTLY WAITING FOR...

....

....

....

....

....

....

....

....

....

....

....

Thank You, Lord,
for hearing my prayers!

*Be joyful in hope,
patient in affliction,
faithful in prayer.*
ROMANS 12:12

DATE ▶

PRAYER REQUESTS:

....
....
....
....
....
....
....
....

ANSWERS TO PRAYER:

....
....
....
....
....
....
....
....
....
....

MY PRAYER FOR TODAY...

....
....
....
....
....
....
....
....
....
....
....
....

AMEN.

PATIENTLY WAITING FOR...

....
....
....
....
....
....
....
....
....
....
....
....
....

Thank You, Lord,
for hearing my prayers!

*I have not stopped giving thanks for you,
remembering you in my prayers.*
EPHESIANS 1:16

DATE ▶

PRAYER REQUESTS:

....
....
....
....
....
....
....
....
....

ANSWERS TO PRAYER:

....
....
....
....
....
....
....
....
....

MY PRAYER FOR TODAY...

....

....

....

....

....

....

....

....

....

....

....

....

AMEN.

PATIENTLY WAITING FOR...

....

....

....

....

....

....

....

....

....

....

....

....

Thank You, Lord,
for hearing my prayers!

*I pray that the eyes of your heart may be
enlightened in order that you may know
the hope to which he has called you.*

EPHESIANS 1:18

DATE ▶

PRAYER REQUESTS:

....

....

....

....

....

....

....

....

ANSWERS TO PRAYER:

....

....

....

....

....

....

....

....

....

....

MY PRAYER FOR TODAY...

....
....
....
....
....
....
....
....
....
....
....

AMEN.

PATIENTLY WAITING FOR...

....
....
....
....
....
....
....
....
....
....
....
....
....

Thank You, Lord,
for hearing my prayers!

*I pray that out of his glorious riches he
may strengthen you with power through
his Spirit in your inner being.*

EPHESIANS 3:16

DATE ▶

PRAYER REQUESTS:

....

....

....

....

....

....

....

....

ANSWERS TO PRAYER:

....

....

....

....

....

....

....

....

....

....

MY PRAYER FOR TODAY...

....

....

....

....

....

....

....

....

....

....

....

....

....

AMEN.

PATIENTLY WAITING FOR...

....

....

....

....

....

....

....

....

....

....

....

....

Thank You, Lord,
for hearing my prayers!

*Be alert and always keep on
praying for all the Lord's people.*
EPHESIANS 6:18

DATE ▶

PRAYER REQUESTS:

ANSWERS TO PRAYER:

MY PRAYER FOR TODAY...

....

....

....

....

....

....

....

....

....

....

....

AMEN.

PATIENTLY WAITING FOR...

....

....

....

....

....

....

....

....

....

....

....

Thank You, Lord,
for hearing my prayers!

I always pray with joy.
PHILIPPIANS 1:4

DATE ▶

PRAYER REQUESTS:

....
....
....
....
....
....
....
....

ANSWERS TO PRAYER:

....
....
....
....
....
....
....
....
....
....

PATIENTLY WAITING FOR...

....
....
....
....
....
....
....
....
....
....
....
....

MY PRAYER FOR TODAY...

....
....
....
....
....
....
....
....
....
....
....

AMEN.

Thank You, Lord,
for hearing my prayers!

*And this is my prayer: that your
love may abound more and more in
knowledge and depth of insight.*

PHILIPPIANS 1:9

DATE ▶

PRAYER REQUESTS:

....

....

....

....

....

....

....

....

ANSWERS TO PRAYER:

....

....

....

....

....

....

....

....

....

....

PATIENTLY WAITING FOR...

....
....
....
....
....
....
....
....
....
....
....
....
....

MY PRAYER FOR TODAY...

....
....
....
....
....
....
....
....
....
....
....
....

AMEN.

Thank You, Lord,
for hearing my prayers!

Since the day we heard about you,
we have not stopped praying for you.
COLOSSIANS 1:9

DATE ▶

PRAYER REQUESTS:

....
....
....
....
....
....
....
....
....

ANSWERS TO PRAYER:

....
....
....
....
....
....
....
....
....
....

MY PRAYER FOR TODAY...

....

....

....

....

....

....

....

....

....

....

AMEN.

PATIENTLY WAITING FOR...

....

....

....

....

....

....

....

....

....

....

....

Thank You, Lord,
for hearing my prayers!

*Is anyone among you in trouble?
Let them pray. Is anyone happy?
Let them sing songs of praise.*

JAMES 5:13

DATE ▶

PRAYER REQUESTS:

ANSWERS TO PRAYER:

MY PRAYER FOR TODAY...

....

....

....

....

....

....

....

....

....

....

....

AMEN.

PATIENTLY WAITING FOR...

....

....

....

....

....

....

....

....

....

....

....

....

....

Thank You, Lord,
for hearing my prayers!

The LORD is my strength and my shield;
my heart trusts in him, and he helps me.
My heart leaps for joy, and with
my song I praise him.

PSALM 28:7

DATE ▶

PRAYER REQUESTS:

....
....
....
....
....
....
....
....
....

ANSWERS TO PRAYER:

....
....
....
....
....
....
....
....
....
....

MY PRAYER FOR TODAY...

....
....
....
....
....
....
....
....
....
....
....
....

AMEN.

PATIENTLY WAITING FOR...

....
....
....
....
....
....
....
....
....
....
....
....
....
....

Thank You, Lord,
for hearing my prayers!

*For what you have done I will always
praise you in the presence of your
faithful people. And I will hope in
your name, for your name is good.*

PSALM 52:9

DATE ▶

PRAYER REQUESTS:

....

....

....

....

....

....

....

....

ANSWERS TO PRAYER:

....

....

....

....

....

....

....

....

....

MY PRAYER FOR TODAY...

....
....
....
....
....
....
....
....
....
....
....
....

AMEN.

PATIENTLY WAITING FOR...

....
....
....
....
....
....
....
....
....
....
....
....

Thank You, Lord,
for hearing my prayers!

Devote yourselves to prayer,
being watchful and thankful.
COLOSSIANS 4:2

PRAYER REQUESTS:

ANSWERS TO PRAYER:

MY PRAYER FOR TODAY...

....
....
....
....
....
....
....
....
....
....
....

AMEN.

PATIENTLY WAITING FOR...

....
....
....
....
....
....
....
....
....
....
....

Thank You, Lord,
for hearing my prayers!

Brothers and sisters, pray for us.
1 Thessalonians 5:25

DATE ▶

PRAYER REQUESTS:

....

....

....

....

....

....

....

....

ANSWERS TO PRAYER:

....

....

....

....

....

....

....

....

....

....

MY PRAYER FOR TODAY...

....

....

....

....

....

....

....

....

....

....

....

....

AMEN.

PATIENTLY WAITING FOR...

....

....

....

....

....

....

....

....

....

....

....

....

Thank You, Lord,
for hearing my prayers!

*We pray. . .so that the name of
our Lord Jesus may be glorified
in you, and you in him.*
2 THESSALONIANS 1:12

DATE ▶

PRAYER REQUESTS:

....

....

....

....

....

....

....

....

ANSWERS TO PRAYER:

....

....

....

....

....

....

....

....

....

MY PRAYER FOR TODAY...

....
....
....
....
....
....
....
....
....
....
....
....
....

AMEN.

PATIENTLY WAITING FOR...

....
....
....
....
....
....
....
....
....
....
....
....
....

Thank You, Lord,
for hearing my prayers!

*Be alert and of sober mind
so that you may pray.*
1 PETER 4:7

DATE ▶

PRAYER REQUESTS:

....
....
....
....
....
....
....
....

ANSWERS TO PRAYER:

....
....
....
....
....
....
....
....
....
....
....

MY PRAYER FOR TODAY...

....

....

....

....

....

....

....

....

....

....

....

....

....

....

AMEN.

PATIENTLY WAITING FOR...

....

....

....

....

....

....

....

....

....

....

....

....

....

Thank You, Lord,
for hearing my prayers!

*I pray that you may enjoy good health
and that all may go well with you.*
3 John 2

DATE ▶

PRAYER REQUESTS:

....

....

....

....

....

....

....

....

ANSWERS TO PRAYER:

....

....

....

....

....

....

....

....

....

MY PRAYER FOR TODAY...

....

....

....

....

....

....

....

....

....

....

....

....

....

AMEN.

PATIENTLY WAITING FOR...

....

....

....

....

....

....

....

....

....

....

....

....

....

Thank You, Lord, for hearing my prayers!

"I desire to speak to the Almighty."
JOB 13:3

DATE ▶

PRAYER REQUESTS:

....

....

....

....

....

....

....

....

ANSWERS TO PRAYER:

....

....

....

....

....

....

....

....

....

MY PRAYER FOR TODAY...

....
....
....
....
....
....
....
....
....
....
....
....

AMEN.

PATIENTLY WAITING FOR...

....
....
....
....
....
....
....
....
....
....
....
....

Thank You, Lord,
for hearing my prayers!

*LORD, you are my God; I will exalt you
and praise your name, for in perfect
faithfulness you have done wonderful
things, things planned long ago.*

ISAIAH 25:1

DATE ▶

PRAYER REQUESTS:

....

....

....

....

....

....

....

....

ANSWERS TO PRAYER:

....

....

....

....

....

....

....

....

....

....

MY PRAYER FOR TODAY...

....

....

....

....

....

....

....

....

....

....

....

....

....

....

AMEN.

PATIENTLY WAITING FOR...

....

....

....

....

....

....

....

....

....

....

....

....

Thank You, Lord,
for hearing my prayers!

*Praise the LORD, my soul; all my
inmost being, praise his holy name.*
PSALM 103:1

DATE ▶

PRAYER REQUESTS:

....

....

....

....

....

....

....

....

....

ANSWERS TO PRAYER:

....

....

....

....

....

....

....

....

....

....

MY PRAYER FOR TODAY...

....

....

....

....

....

....

....

....

....

....

....

....

....

AMEN.

PATIENTLY WAITING FOR...

....

....

....

....

....

....

....

....

....

....

....

....

Thank You, Lord,
for hearing my prayers!

My mouth is filled with your praise,
declaring your splendor all day long.
PSALM 71:8

DATE ▶

PRAYER REQUESTS:

ANSWERS TO PRAYER:

MY PRAYER FOR TODAY...

....
....
....
....
....
....
....
....
....
....
....
....
....
....

AMEN.

PATIENTLY WAITING FOR...

....
....
....
....
....
....
....
....
....
....
....
....

Thank You, Lord,
for hearing my prayers!

Because your love is better than life,
my lips will glorify you.
PSALM 63:3

DATE ▶

PRAYER REQUESTS:

....

....

....

....

....

....

....

....

ANSWERS TO PRAYER:

....

....

....

....

....

....

....

....

....

....

MY PRAYER FOR TODAY...

....
....
....
....
....
....
....
....
....
....
....
....
....
....

AMEN.

PATIENTLY WAITING FOR...

....
....
....
....
....
....
....
....
....
....
....
....
....
....
....
....

Thank You, Lord, for hearing my prayers!

Great is the LORD and most worthy of praise;
his greatness no one can fathom.

PSALM 145:3

DATE ▶

PRAYER REQUESTS:

....
....
....
....
....
....
....
....

ANSWERS TO PRAYER:

....
....
....
....
....
....
....
....
....
....

MY PRAYER FOR TODAY...

....
....
....
....
....
....
....
....
....
....
....
....
....
....

AMEN.

PATIENTLY WAITING FOR...

....
....
....
....
....
....
....
....
....
....
....
....
....

Thank You, Lord,
for hearing my prayers!

*You, Lord, are forgiving and good,
abounding in love to all who call to you.*
PSALM 86:5

DATE ▶

PRAYER REQUESTS:

....
....
....
....
....
....
....
....
....

ANSWERS TO PRAYER:

....
....
....
....
....
....
....
....
....
....

MY PRAYER FOR TODAY...

....
....
....
....
....
....
....
....
....
....

AMEN.

PATIENTLY WAITING FOR...

....
....
....
....
....
....
....
....
....
....
....
....

Thank You, Lord,
for hearing my prayers!

*Trust in the LORD with all your heart
and lean not on your own understanding.*
PROVERBS 3:5

DATE ▶

PRAYER REQUESTS:

....
....
....
....
....
....
....
....
....

ANSWERS TO PRAYER:

....
....
....
....
....
....
....
....
....
....
....

MY PRAYER FOR TODAY...

....

....

....

....

....

....

....

....

....

....

....

....

....

AMEN.

PATIENTLY WAITING FOR...

....

....

....

....

....

....

....

....

....

....

....

....

....

....

Thank You, Lord, for hearing my prayers!

I sought the LORD, and he answered me;
he delivered me from all my fears.
PSALM 34:4

DATE ▶

PRAYER REQUESTS:

....
....
....
....
....
....
....
....

ANSWERS TO PRAYER:

....
....
....
....
....
....
....
....
....
....
....

MY PRAYER FOR TODAY...

....
....
....
....
....
....
....
....
....
....
....
....

AMEN.

PATIENTLY WAITING FOR...

....
....
....
....
....
....
....
....
....
....
....
....
....

Thank You, Lord,
for hearing my prayers!

I will praise you with an upright heart
as I learn your righteous laws.
PSALM 119:7

DATE ▶

PRAYER REQUESTS:

....
....
....
....
....
....
....
....
....

ANSWERS TO PRAYER:

....
....
....
....
....
....
....
....
....
....

MY PRAYER FOR TODAY...

....
....
....
....
....
....
....
....
....
....
....
....

AMEN.

PATIENTLY WAITING FOR...

....
....
....
....
....
....
....
....
....
....
....
....
....
....

Thank You, Lord,
for hearing my prayers!

*And my God will meet all your
needs according to the riches
of his glory in Christ Jesus.*

PHILIPPIANS 4:19

DATE ▶

PRAYER REQUESTS:

....
....
....
....
....
....
....
....
....
....

ANSWERS TO PRAYER:

....
....
....
....
....
....
....
....
....
....

MY PRAYER FOR TODAY...

....

....

....

....

....

....

....

....

....

....

....

AMEN.

PATIENTLY WAITING FOR...

....

....

....

....

....

....

....

....

....

....

....

....

....

Thank You, Lord,
for hearing my prayers!

But thanks be to God!
He gives us the victory through
our Lord Jesus Christ.
1 CORINTHIANS 15:57

DATE ▶

PRAYER REQUESTS:

....

....

....

....

....

....

....

....

ANSWERS TO PRAYER:

....

....

....

....

....

....

....

....

....

....

MY PRAYER FOR TODAY...

....

....

....

....

....

....

....

....

....

....

....

....

....

AMEN.

PATIENTLY WAITING FOR...

....

....

....

....

....

....

....

....

....

....

....

....

Thank You, Lord,
for hearing my prayers!

I cry to you, LORD; I say,
"You are my refuge, my portion
in the land of the living."
PSALM 142:5

DATE ▶

PRAYER REQUESTS:

ANSWERS TO PRAYER:

MY PRAYER FOR TODAY...

....
....
....
....
....
....
....
....
....
....
....

AMEN.

PATIENTLY WAITING FOR...

....
....
....
....
....
....
....
....
....
....
....
....
....

Thank You, Lord,
for hearing my prayers!

*Give thanks to the LORD,
for he is good;
his love endures forever.*
1 CHRONICLES 16:34

DATE ▶

PRAYER REQUESTS:

....
....
....
....
....
....
....
....
....

ANSWERS TO PRAYER:

....
....
....
....
....
....
....
....
....
....

MY PRAYER FOR TODAY...

....

....

....

....

....

....

....

....

....

....

....

....

....

AMEN.

PATIENTLY WAITING FOR...

....

....

....

....

....

....

....

....

....

....

....

....

Thank You, Lord,
for hearing my prayers!

*Praise be to the Lord,
to God our Savior,
who daily bears our burdens.*

PSALM 68:19

PRAYER REQUESTS:

....
....
....
....
....
....
....
....
....

ANSWERS TO PRAYER:

....
....
....
....
....
....
....
....
....
....

MY PRAYER FOR TODAY...

....
....
....
....
....
....
....
....
....
....
....
....

AMEN.

PATIENTLY WAITING FOR...

....
....
....
....
....
....
....
....
....
....
....
....
....

Thank You, Lord,
for hearing my prayers!

*"To him who sits on the throne and to
the Lamb be praise and honor and glory
and power, for ever and ever!"*
REVELATION 5:13

DATE ▶

PRAYER REQUESTS:

....
....
....
....
....
....
....
....
....

ANSWERS TO PRAYER:

....
....
....
....
....
....
....
....
....

MY PRAYER FOR TODAY...

....
....
....
....
....
....
....
....
....
....
....
....
....
....

AMEN.

PATIENTLY WAITING FOR...

....
....
....
....
....
....
....
....
....
....
....
....
....
....

Thank You, Lord,
for hearing my prayers!

*"But blessed is the one
who trusts in the LORD,
whose confidence is in him."*
JEREMIAH 17:7

DATE ▶

PRAYER REQUESTS:

....

....

....

....

....

....

....

....

ANSWERS TO PRAYER:

....

....

....

....

....

....

....

....

....

MY PRAYER FOR TODAY...

....

....

....

....

....

....

....

....

....

....

....

....

....

AMEN.

PATIENTLY WAITING FOR...

....

....

....

....

....

....

....

....

....

....

....

....

....

....

Thank You, Lord,
for hearing my prayers!

*May the God of hope fill you with all
joy and peace as you trust in him,
so that you may overflow with hope
by the power of the Holy Spirit.*

ROMANS 15:13

DATE ▶

PRAYER REQUESTS:

....
....
....
....
....
....
....
....
....

ANSWERS TO PRAYER:

....
....
....
....
....
....
....
....
....
....

MY PRAYER FOR TODAY...

....
....
....
....
....
....
....
....
....
....
....

AMEN.

PATIENTLY WAITING FOR...

....
....
....
....
....
....
....
....
....
....
....
....
....
....

Thank You, Lord,
for hearing my prayers!

As for me, I will always have hope;
I will praise you more and more.
PSALM 71:14

DATE ▶

PRAYER REQUESTS:

....

....

....

....

....

....

....

....

ANSWERS TO PRAYER:

....

....

....

....

....

....

....

....

....

....

MY PRAYER FOR TODAY...

....

....

....

....

....

....

....

....

....

....

....

....

....

AMEN.

PATIENTLY WAITING FOR...

....

....

....

....

....

....

....

....

....

....

....

....

....

....

....

Thank You, Lord,
for hearing my prayers!

*Let us hold unswervingly to
the hope we profess,
for he who promised is faithful.*
HEBREWS 10:23

DATE ▶

PRAYER REQUESTS:

....
....
....
....
....
....
....
....
....

ANSWERS TO PRAYER:

....
....
....
....
....
....
....
....
....
....

MY PRAYER FOR TODAY...

....

....

....

....

....

....

....

....

....

....

....

....

....

AMEN.

PATIENTLY WAITING FOR...

....

....

....

....

....

....

....

....

....

....

....

....

....

....

Thank You, Lord, for hearing my prayers!

"Blessed is the one who trusts in the LORD, whose confidence is in him."

JEREMIAH 17:7

DATE ▶

PRAYER REQUESTS:

....
....
....
....
....
....
....
....
....

ANSWERS TO PRAYER:

....
....
....
....
....
....
....
....
....
....
....

PATIENTLY WAITING FOR...

....
....
....
....
....
....
....
....
....
....
....
....
....

MY PRAYER FOR TODAY...

....
....
....
....
....
....
....
....
....
....
....
....
....
....

AMEN.

Thank You, Lord,
for hearing my prayers!

*May your unfailing love be with us,
Lord, even as we put our hope in you.*
PSALM 33:22

DATE ▶

PRAYER REQUESTS:

....
....
....
....
....
....
....
....
....

ANSWERS TO PRAYER:

....
....
....
....
....
....
....
....
....

MY PRAYER FOR TODAY...

....

....

....

....

....

....

....

....

....

....

....

....

....

AMEN.

PATIENTLY WAITING FOR...

....

....

....

....

....

....

....

....

....

....

....

....

....

Thank You, Lord,
for hearing my prayers!

"Be still, and know that I am God;
I will be exalted among the nations,
I will be exalted in the earth."

PSALM 46:10

DATE ▶

PRAYER REQUESTS:

....

....

....

....

....

....

....

....

....

ANSWERS TO PRAYER:

....

....

....

....

....

....

....

....

....

MY PRAYER FOR TODAY...

....

....

....

....

....

....

....

....

....

....

....

....

AMEN.

PATIENTLY WAITING FOR...

....

....

....

....

....

....

....

....

....

....

....

....

....

Thank You, Lord,
for hearing my prayers!

*"He is my refuge and my fortress,
my God, in whom I trust."*

PSALM 91:2

DATE ▶

PRAYER REQUESTS:

....
....
....
....
....
....
....
....
....

ANSWERS TO PRAYER:

....
....
....
....
....
....
....
....
....
....

MY PRAYER FOR TODAY...

....

....

....

....

....

....

....

....

....

....

....

....

AMEN.

PATIENTLY WAITING FOR...

....

....

....

....

....

....

....

....

....

....

....

....

....

Thank You, Lord,
for hearing my prayers!

He who watches over you will not slumber.
PSALM 121:3

DATE ▶

PRAYER REQUESTS:

....
....
....
....
....
....
....
....
....

ANSWERS TO PRAYER:

....
....
....
....
....
....
....
....
....

MY PRAYER FOR TODAY...

....
....
....
....
....
....
....
....
....
....
....
....
....

AMEN.

PATIENTLY WAITING FOR...

....
....
....
....
....
....
....
....
....
....
....
....
....

Thank You, Lord,
for hearing my prayers!

*Wait for the LORD; be strong and
take heart and wait for the LORD.*
PSALM 27:14

DATE ▶

PRAYER REQUESTS:

....
....
....
....
....
....
....
....
....

ANSWERS TO PRAYER:

....
....
....
....
....
....
....
....
....

MY PRAYER FOR TODAY...

....

....

....

....

....

....

....

....

....

....

....

AMEN.

PATIENTLY WAITING FOR...

....

....

....

....

....

....

....

....

....

....

....

....

Thank You, Lord,
for hearing my prayers!

*Keep me safe, my God,
for in you I take refuge.*
PSALM 16:1

DATE ▶

PRAYER REQUESTS:

....

....

....

....

....

....

....

....

....

....

ANSWERS TO PRAYER:

....

....

....

....

....

....

....

....

....

....

MY PRAYER FOR TODAY...

....

....

....

....

....

....

....

....

....

....

....

AMEN.

PATIENTLY WAITING FOR...

....

....

....

....

....

....

....

....

....

....

....

....

Thank You, Lord,
for hearing my prayers!

*"Truly I tell you, if you have faith as small as
a mustard seed, you can say to this mountain,
'Move from here to there,' and it will move.
Nothing will be impossible for you."*

MATTHEW 17:20

PRAYER REQUESTS:

....

....

....

....

....

....

....

....

ANSWERS TO PRAYER:

....

....

....

....

....

....

....

....

....

....

MY PRAYER FOR TODAY...

....
....
....
....
....
....
....
....
....
....
....

AMEN.

PATIENTLY WAITING FOR...

....
....
....
....
....
....
....
....
....
....
....

Thank You, Lord,
for hearing my prayers!

*I remain confident of this: I will see the
goodness of the LORD in the land of the living.*
PSALM 27:13

DATE ▶

PRAYER REQUESTS:

....
....
....
....
....
....
....
....
....

ANSWERS TO PRAYER:

....
....
....
....
....
....
....
....
....
....

MY PRAYER FOR TODAY...

....
....
....
....
....
....
....
....
....
....
....
....

AMEN.

PATIENTLY WAITING FOR...

....
....
....
....
....
....
....
....
....
....
....
....

Thank You, Lord,
for hearing my prayers!

*"Ask and you will receive,
and your joy will be complete."*
John 16:24

DATE ▶

PRAYER REQUESTS:

....

....

....

....

....

....

....

....

....

ANSWERS TO PRAYER:

....

....

....

....

....

....

....

....

....

....

MY PRAYER FOR TODAY...

....
....
....
....
....
....
....
....
....
....
....
....

AMEN.

PATIENTLY WAITING FOR...

....
....
....
....
....
....
....
....
....
....
....

Thank You, Lord,
for hearing my prayers!

*If any of you lacks wisdom,
you should ask God, who gives
generously to all without finding
fault, and it will be given to you.*

JAMES 1:5

DATE ▶

PRAYER REQUESTS:

....
....
....
....
....
....
....
....

ANSWERS TO PRAYER:

....
....
....
....
....
....
....
....
....
....

MY PRAYER FOR TODAY...

....
....
....
....
....
....
....
....
....
....
....
....
....

AMEN.

PATIENTLY WAITING FOR...

....
....
....
....
....
....
....
....
....
....
....
....

Thank You, Lord,
for hearing my prayers!

And God is able to bless you abundantly.
2 CORINTHIANS 9:8

DATE ▶

PRAYER REQUESTS:

....
....
....
....
....
....
....
....
....

ANSWERS TO PRAYER:

....
....
....
....
....
....
....
....
....
....

MY PRAYER FOR TODAY...

....

....

....

....

....

....

....

....

....

....

....

....

....

AMEN.

PATIENTLY WAITING FOR...

....

....

....

....

....

....

....

....

....

....

....

....

....

Thank You, Lord,
for hearing my prayers!

He who did not spare his own Son,
but gave him up for us all—
how will he not also, along with him,
graciously give us all things?

ROMANS 8:32

DATE ▶

PRAYER REQUESTS:

....

....

....

....

....

....

....

....

....

....

ANSWERS TO PRAYER:

....

....

....

....

....

....

....

....

....

....

MY PRAYER FOR TODAY...

....

....

....

....

....

....

....

....

....

....

....

AMEN.

PATIENTLY WAITING FOR...

....

....

....

....

....

....

....

....

....

....

....

....

Thank You, Lord, for hearing my prayers!

His divine power has given us everything we need for a godly life through our knowledge of him who called us by his own glory and goodness.

2 PETER 1:3

DATE ▶

PRAYER REQUESTS:

....
....
....
....
....
....
....
....

ANSWERS TO PRAYER:

....
....
....
....
....
....
....
....
....
....

MY PRAYER FOR TODAY...

....
....
....
....
....
....
....
....
....
....
....
....

AMEN.

PATIENTLY WAITING FOR...

....
....
....
....
....
....
....
....
....
....
....

Thank You, Lord,
for hearing my prayers!

*Faith is confidence in what we hope for
and assurance about what we do not see.*
HEBREWS 11:1

DATE ▶

PRAYER REQUESTS:

....
....
....
....
....
....
....
....

ANSWERS TO PRAYER:

....
....
....
....
....
....
....
....
....
....

MY PRAYER FOR TODAY...

....

....

....

....

....

....

....

....

....

....

....

AMEN.

PATIENTLY WAITING FOR...

....

....

....

....

....

....

....

....

....

....

....

Thank You, Lord,
for hearing my prayers!

*You are God my Savior,
and my hope is in you all day long.*

PSALM 25:5

DATE ▶

PRAYER REQUESTS:

....
....
....
....
....
....
....
....

ANSWERS TO PRAYER:

....
....
....
....
....
....
....
....
....
....

MY PRAYER FOR TODAY...

....
....
....
....
....
....
....
....
....
....
....

AMEN.

PATIENTLY WAITING FOR...

....
....
....
....
....
....
....
....
....
....
....
....

Thank You, Lord,
for hearing my prayers!

*"Ask and it will be given to you; seek and
you will find; knock and the door will be
opened to you. For everyone who asks receives;
the one who seeks finds; and to the one
who knocks, the door will be opened."*

MATTHEW 7:7–8

DATE ▶

PRAYER REQUESTS:

....
....
....
....
....
....
....
....

ANSWERS TO PRAYER:

....
....
....
....
....
....
....
....
....
....

MY PRAYER FOR TODAY...

....
....
....
....
....
....
....
....
....
....
....
....
....

AMEN.

PATIENTLY WAITING FOR...

....
....
....
....
....
....
....
....
....
....
....
....

Thank You, Lord,
for hearing my prayers!

Answer me when I call to you,
my righteous God.
PSALM 4:1

DATE ▶

PRAYER REQUESTS:

....
....
....
....
....
....
....
....

ANSWERS TO PRAYER:

....
....
....
....
....
....
....
....
....

MY PRAYER FOR TODAY...

....
....
....
....
....
....
....
....
....
....
....
....
....

AMEN.

PATIENTLY WAITING FOR...

....
....
....
....
....
....
....
....
....
....
....
....

Thank You, Lord, for hearing my prayers!

The Lord. . .is faithful in all he does.
PSALM 33:4

DATE ▶

PRAYER REQUESTS:

....
....
....
....
....
....
....
....
....
....

ANSWERS TO PRAYER:

....
....
....
....
....
....
....
....
....
....

MY PRAYER FOR TODAY...

....
....
....
....
....
....
....
....
....
....
....
....
....

AMEN.

PATIENTLY WAITING FOR...

....
....
....
....
....
....
....
....
....
....
....
....
....
....

Thank You, Lord,
for hearing my prayers!

Pray continually.
1 THESSALONIANS 5:17

The Prayer Map® for the Entire Family. . .

*The Prayer Map
for Men*
978-1-64352-438-2

*The Prayer Map
for Women*
978-1-68322-557-7

*The Prayer Map
for Girls*
978-1-68322-559-1

*The Prayer Map
for Boys*
978-1-68322-558-4

*The Prayer Map
for Teens*
978-1-68322-556-0

These purposeful prayer journals are a fun and creative way to more fully experience the power of prayer. Each page guides you to write out thoughts, ideas, and lists. . .which then creates a specific "map" for you to follow as you talk to God. Each map includes a spot to record the date, so you can look back on your prayers and see how God has worked in your life. *The Prayer Map* will not only encourage you to spend time talking with God about the things that matter most. . .it will also help you build a healthy spiritual habit of continual prayer for life!

Spiral Bound / $7.99

*Find These and More from Barbour Books
at Your Favorite Bookstore*
www.barbourbooks.com